RV Hacks:
Guide On Cheap&Easy RV Traveling All Over The USA

Disclamer: All photos used in this book, including the cover photo were made available under a Attribution-NonCommercial-ShareAlike 2.0 Generic and sourced from Flickr

Copyright 2016 by publisher - All rights reserved.

This document is geared towards providing exact and reliable information in regards to the topic and issue covered. The publication is sold with the idea that the publisher is not required to render accounting, officially permitted, or otherwise, qualified services. If advice is necessary, legal or professional, a practiced individual in the profession should be ordered.

- From a Declaration of Principles which was accepted and approved equally by a Committee of the American Bar Association and a Committee of Publishers and Associations.

In no way is it legal to reproduce, duplicate, or transmit any part of this document in either electronic means or in printed format. Recording of this publication is strictly prohibited and any storage of this document is not allowed unless with written permission from the publisher. All rights reserved.

The information provided herein is stated to be truthful and consistent, in that any liability, in terms of inattention or otherwise, by any usage or abuse of any policies, processes, or directions contained within is the solitary and utter responsibility of the recipient reader. Under no circumstances will any legal responsibility or blame be held against the publisher for any reparation, damages, or monetary loss due to the information herein, either directly or indirectly.

Respective authors own all copyrights not held by the publisher.

The information herein is offered for informational purposes solely, and is universal as so. The presentation of the information is without contract or any type of guarantee assurance.

The trademarks that are used are without any consent, and the publication of the trademark is without permission or backing by the trademark owner. All trademarks and brands within this book are for clarifying purposes only and are the owned by the owners themselves, not affiliated with this document.

Table of content

RV Hacks: 1

   Guide On Cheap&Easy RV Traveling All Over The USA...1

Introduction 5

Chapter 1: RV travelling for Beginners 6

Chapter 2: Secrets to getting the best camping sites 11

Chapter 3: Basic steps to plan your RV trip...15

Chapter 4: How to prepare your RV for a trip and make a perfect route to travel all over the USA21

Conclusions..27

Introduction

In the Northern part of USA, there are these vehicles, RV (Recreational Vehicle), that always come with amenities found in a typical home. They are just normal motor vehicles that have features such as bathroom, kitchen as well as one or two sleeping facilities. While a good number of the RVs are single-deck, there are others also that come as double-deck.

Ideally, RVs,, also referred to as **motorhomes**, are specially intended for leisure activities, like **camping** and going for **vacations**. This means therefore, that there are some specific places where they can be found, such as in the **campgrounds** and in the **RV camps**. They can always be rented in major cities by business travellers, who use them as mobile offices for businesses. This is always convenient as they have some customizations such as *satellite internet, an electrical system(upgraded)*, an *extra desk space* and a *generator*. Apart from the business purposes, RVs are also rented by tourists.

RV camping is indeed great! It does not only let you enjoy the great adventure, but also a wonderful and a fantastic way to help you leave behind all your worries. There are those who use the RVs as travelling permanent homes on a full-time basis. They can be a retired couple, or just a family going for vacation. These people are commonly known as '*full-timers*'. If you are new to RV and wondering how to find the great campsites and locations, how to plan for the trips and any other thing, do not worry. Simply click through the pages in this book and find yourself in any destination you want to go to.

Chapter 1: RV travelling for Beginners

RV (also known as recreational vehicle)has today become very popular, especially among retirees. One of the greatest reason why it is becoming widespread is the flexibility and the freedom it offers the RVers. For instance, if you get to a place and like it, you can stay there for as long as you want. And, if you feel you've overstayed the place, you simply pack your belongings and move to another place.

RV has also become a darling to many, including business men who travel from one place to another for business purposes, basically due to its affordability. Many people today like traveling using planes and such like means. Considering rental costs for example, travelling using RV is much more cheaper and convenient than it is by a car or even a plane. This is very evident when you bring to considerations factors such as *restaurant* and *lodging* costs.

Whether a retired couple or a whole family of weekend campers who desire to travel as full-timers, there are some important things that every beginner has to be aware of. As a beginner, you may find them very difficult to fathom. However, you get so used to them and find them very easy to apply overtime.

These are some of the steps you can consider as a beginner before you head out with your RV.

1) **Make a choice between buying and renting**

Making a choice of whether you want to buy or rent the RV is very important. It is however not as easy as one may probably think since both have their merits and demerits. There are factors that still can help you in making such a crucial decision.

If travelling using RV for the first time, consider renting as this will help determine the RV that will accommodate your needs best. If planning a single trip also, it is advisable that you rent. Renting generally helps you to determine whether you want to continue shelling out the money to rent or will consider purchasing for the future trips.

However, if you are a retired couple and are foreseeing yourselves going for a full-time RV camping, consider buying an RV. This will help so much when it comes to cost as well as convenience matters.

Cost is another important factor to be considered when making a decision of buying or renting an RV. Depending on the RV you choose, the costs for renting vary.

2) **Take a drive test**

Before going out to the trip, take some short-distant trips on the road you'll use. There are some things that as a first timer you will need to know. Once you know the details in driving, you'll have no problem when it comes to making changes (if there be any). One of the changes you'll have known how to make is closing the drawers, which normally pop open.

3) **Have full knowledge of your RV**

Every RV beginner, whether using a rented or a bought RV, should have full knowledge of the RV. This means that before planning any trip, get to know all the interiors and exteriors of the RV. If for instance it has a problem, ensure that you are able to evaluate and also fix it permanently. When you do this on a regular basis, you'll be able to save not only cash but also your time, which you would have spent at a mechanic.

Also, when you fully understand your motorhome, there's less probability of you causing operational mistakes. For example, if you already know the number of amps your main breaker can handle, then you're on the safe side. Without this understanding, you can easily blow the breaker up.

4) **Forget not your tools and spares**

With RVs, irrespective of how strong they're made, you'll always need to carry your spares and tools along. This is because there are certain things that will have to be cut, loosened, fixed and even tightened. Things such as jumper cables, bulbs, bolts, connectors, nuts and other extra fuses should always be stocked in your tool kit.

5) **Ensure you have a campground set-up checklist**

Any beginner who still has no campground routine is advised to come up with a checklist. This is important as the checklist will make sure that everything is set up and runs just as it ought to be.

6) **Make sure also that you do not wing**

Just as a checklist is important, having a plan that guides you in the course of the trip is equally important. Many times, when in the trip, there's always the desire to go to any place you want. Having the plan will help guide you to stick to the budget you had, identify the stopping areas (the sites and the places you'd want to look at), know the terrain of the route you'll take and what to do about it, carry enough food for the family for entire period and even identify the campground, where you'll stop and spend the night.

With all the above guidelines, it is evident that RV beginners really have lots of things to put into place. In order to enjoy stress-free trips, it's important that the preparations be started as early as possible, with the guidelines followed to the latter. If you are planning one, just ensure you follow these basics keenly, and you will be glad you did.

Chapter 2: Secrets to getting the best camping sites

There's nothing as frustrating as walking all over just looking for a suitable campsite. However even though it frustrates, it's worth it. just imagine an instance where, together with your family or spouse, you are enjoying your wonderful and peaceful sleep in your RV, just for your sleep to be interrupted by the campground hosts. That is the worst thing that can happen to you when outdoors, camping with your family.

Well, that tells just one thing; no matter how picturesque the view is, or how beautiful the campground is, your trip will in the end not be enjoyable as you probably expected it to be if you have pitched your camp in a wrong place.

The only way to get the best campground is to carry out prior planning. It is the most critical thing when camping. Planning process starts when you're still at home and ends when you get back home. Many have always thought that it begins when you reach the campground. This way, you'll be damn messed up since you'll realise the many things you haven't put in place. The most important part in planning involves getting the top-notch RV campground that will satisfy all your longings. This, you can be sure, can make every member of your group have a delightful experience.

How then can you get such a campground?

- Ask for a detailed map: If you get to a place, especially an unfamiliar campground, ask for a detailed map from the campground hosts. With the help of the map, quickly drive around the area to check and make a list of possible campsite locations you have identified. This will help you make a sound decision concerning the suitable site.

- Do not pick a site just because it has camping items: Many have settled in a place they thought was suitable just because of the camping items they found there, only to be evicted later by the owners. If you find a place that has camping items but no vehicles, this could mean that the owners are just away for some time, but will definitely get back.

- Punctuality matters a lot when looking for a suitable campground. Normally, the best time to look for a campground is morning hours. So, to be on the safe side, arrive as early as possible.

- Water is a great RV's enemy. Hence, make sure you camp in a dry place, at least 200-300 feet away from water. Also, setting up the camp away from water is important as it keeps insects, e.g. *mosquitoes* at bay. If it is a rainy season, set up camp where water flows away from your site. Nevertheless, water is critical. Ensure that you choose a camp site that is near a water source. This is because you will need the water for drinking, cooking and even washing.

- Also, when looking for a campsite, look for a place that has sun shelter. However, if rain is anticipated, do not set up your camp under trees (especially the big pine trees). This is because of the danger of lightening, as well as the fact that trees, even long after the rains have stopped, will continue to rain on your site.

- Find a place that is free from rocks or roots. If for instance you've found an ideal area but has a problem with the small rocks, simply clear them with a rake, to create a level ground for sleeping on.

- Resist the temptation of sharing a site with other campers who are not part of you. This is a time for you and your family to enjoy every little thing you experience. Sharing may not be the best thing as some campers may want to join in all your activities, while you need your privacy.

- Do not set up your camp near wild animals or near the source of their food. Trust me, they'll always be a bother.

- Since it a place away from home, it is always good to be ready for anything. For this reason, look for an area that has a source of firewood in its surrounding. It may not be necessary because you may end up not using the firewood, but important anyway.

- Also, if you have identified a certain site, ensure it is large enough to accomodate and meet all your needs.

Now, the most important thing is finding the best camping site. This is why I talked of having prior planning. This is not the time to do things in a hurry to meet deadline or with impatience. It is the moment you should take ample time to ensure you fall in the right place (that is if you want to have a pleasurable experience).

Chapter 3: Basic steps to plan your RV trip

Since it came to be, many families are now viewing RVing as the best way ever to travel and have fun as a family. RVs come with everything you'll need while on the trip. Such include the cheaply priced campgrounds to park at and a comfortable place to rest, giving you a greater way to spend your quality time with your family.

Planning is the most important thing you have to do when considering to go to an RV trip. In this chapter, I want to discuss some basic steps you should follow before heading out.

1) Outline your route

Before hitting the open road, you've got to outline your routes clearly. It is here that you will determine whether you want to take a scenic route with beautiful sites to view, or just a normal route without so many things that can distract your journey. Some families normally choose the latter, especially when they want to reach their destination early. Also, when outlining your routes, make sure you consider the time and the season of the year. Summer trips, for instance are always more flexible than the winter trips, which are best done in the Southern part of the country.

2) Create timeline

This becomes very easy if you have known the route you are going to take. Creating timeline will enable you know the far you'll always be driving every single day. It will also cover the time you'd want to reach your destination as well as the roadside attractions that you'd wish to stop and have a look at. Remember RV is all about adventure. You therefore should always leave room to sightsee along the journey as well as time to stretch your legs.

3) Create your budget

Coming up with a budget will help you determine the number of times you'll always be eating out, the money you will spend in case there's an emergency, as well as the groceries you'll buy. With the varied prices of the RV parks and the campgrounds, a well built budget will help you determine the ones you can afford to stay at.

4) Purchase of RV insurance

Insurance is another important thing you should consider having before you set the trip. If you are on a long RV trip for instance, you'd want to be certain that your rig plus all that is in it is pretty safe in case an accident occurs. Although only a few insurance companies do cover the motorhomes, you can just get in touch with your auto insurance company to add RV to your current policy.

5) Know your electrical load

RVs cannot run all appliances at the same time. Knowing your electrical load is essential as it will keep the RV up and running and your family safe as well. To help you run your chores effectively in the RV, simply label your appliances in order to be aware of the total power usage. If for example, your RV is 40 amps, label your appliances with the number of appliances they draw. e.g. a toaster can be 10 amps and egg cooker, 10 amps. This means that when making breakfast, you may not run the 20 amp air conditioner.

6) Make a Checklist

Since you'll be away from home, ensure that you have a checklist for all items you'll need on board. Even though you can get some of the supplies along the way, you can as well save your time and money by packing everything you'll need to start with. The importance of a checklist is simply that you have even the most obvious things, which may be handy whenever you need them.

Some of the important things that have to be included in your list are such as:

a) *Food supply*

This is the most important section whenever planning a long RV trip. Since most RVs normally have room for storage as well as cooking space, you can pack all the supplies you'll need while on the trip.

b) *Sleeping*

RV trips, as we all know, are always full of fun. With these, its always good to start the morning refreshed. You can enjoy a good night's sleep by opening the windows during the night to avoid the suffocation, or even set the air/heat in order to enjoy your sleep in any given weather. The following are the basic things to carry along;

- *Extra blankets and/or sleeping bag(s)*
- *Bed sheets for all the beds*
- *Pillows and pillow cases*

c) *Relaxing*

Being a trip full of activities here and there, it would be very important to set aside some time for rest and relaxation.

In your checklist, include the following (but are not limited to these) things to use during this time.

- *Cards and games*
- *Pens and paper*
- *Books to read*
- *Lawn games*
- *Crossword puzzles*

d) **Bathing**

One thing you will agree with me is that you'll need to wash off the outdoor play and the sweat. This you can do by staying warm and clean with the actual bathroom available in your RV.

The following will have to feature in your list in this category

- *Towels*
- *Soap*
- *Toothbrush and toothpaste*
- *Toiletry kit*
- *Toilet paper*
- *Shampoo and conditioner*

e) **RV Essentials**

Anything can always happen in a journey. To be on the safe side while still away from home, ensure that you pack maintenance items and tools such as the following (not limited to these however);

- *Batteries*
- *Extension cords*
- *A pair of Scissors*
- *Gloves*
- *Flashlights*
- *First Aid Kit*
- *Insect repellant*
- *Comfortable shoes*
- *Fire extinguisher*

7) **Pack in stages**

There's nothing as overwhelming as trying to pack everything all at once. To make your work easier and even enjoyable, take a week and pack something new each day. For instance, you can take one day to pack all kitchen/food supplies that you'll need. The following day, you can tackle games and items that will keep children entertained. You can continue with this, daily, until you pack everything. The problem with trying to pack everything all at once is that you are likely forget some important things.

8) **Manage the RV weight**

Coordinate your packing with the legal weight of your RV. After packing everything, get to a commercial truck weigh station and weigh your RV. If found overloaded, unload the unnecessary items first till its even. The easiest way of lightening the load is, instead of storing water and fuel in the rig, get them at each stop you make. It will greatly help minimize the excess weight.

9) **Inspect roads and check weather conditions**

On the material day, when leaving for the trip, check the weather conditions and be ready to alter your route and timeline, when necessary. In order to avoid any uncalled-for condition, ensure you do a quick check to every single morning before hitting the road. With these, you can be sure to have a wonderful plan that will make your trip enjoyable.

Chapter 4: How to prepare your RV for a trip and make a perfect route to travel all over the USA

Just recently we were planning a family trip to Florida. I remember how my kids were jumping around like little calves, on hearing that we would be travelling the following weekend. It sounded to them as the news of the year. As kids would do, they started telling and inviting some of their friends to go with us.

Meanwhile, my husband and I were pulling strings together to plan the best and effective way possible, so as to enjoy it to the fullest, given that this was going to be our first RV trip ever. Since we never wanted to miss out on anything, we sought information from some of our friends who had gone several times. Thanks to our friend, Craig, who was always there on time to help us with everything we needed to know ahead of time.

Craig made us learn lots of things. I remember how he gave us a checklist, which he said would be of great help to us during the trip. He took my husband through some steps, which apparently, we were to do before heading out to our trip. I realised it really involved a lot, especially if you are going with a bigger group. However, one thing that Craig assured us was the pleasure we'll experience once we head out. Oh! My God! I couldn't just wait for that!

You definitely want to have an awesome experience, come back safe and sound so that you go back another time, right? Look at the following ways of preparing your RV for a trip and make a perfect route to travel all over the USA.

1) **Exterior**

Normally, after the winter season, there's too much water leaks, which greatly affects the RV. To keep this in check, do a thorough check on your roof and the caulking, primarily around the windows, vents, air conditioners as well as the doors, to ensure that the cracks and the caulk are all intact. Since water is among the biggest troubles of the RV, ensure that even the smallest cracks as well as holes are well sealed.

2) **Tires**

Another important part that you need to seriously inspect is the tires. On tires, carefully inspect the sidewall cracks or those found between the treads. If noticed, treat the cracks with all seriousness and, if necessary, replace the tires. When replacing a tire, refer to the manufacturer's manual. Apart from the manual, there should also be some recommended tire pressures from the decal inside of a cabinet.

3) **Batteries**

There's nothing as frustrating as going to a camping trip with spoilt batteries. So as not to get into any mess, ensure you inspect all your batteries before setting out to any camping trip, to be sure they are in a good condition. When doing this, wear protective gears such as latex or protective gloves and safety glasses. When checking the batteries, make sure that the main power switch, the shore power and some other items in the RV are switched off.

The corroded terminals, batteries as well as connections need also to be checked and thoroughly cleaned. You can use hot water and baking soda for the cleaning. Battery fluid levels also need to be checked. There are certain battery caps that aren't always removed. However, you can as well remove and take back each in its place.

The first ever camping trip is always the best time to test your batteries. To test them, fully charge them first then take to a professional to perform the load test. Charging them before the test is very important, since, if you take them to the test without charging, they'll definitely fail the test.

Battery replacement is another important thing you need to consider. Any time you want to replace your batteries, make sure you replace the multiple battery banks together. Adding an old battery to a new one isn't advisable. Chassis batteries, for example, and Coach batteries, are always banked separately.

4) **Water**

Before you fill the hot water heater bypass valve with water, ensure you check it first. With all the faucets closed, the valve should be in its normal state. To fill up your RV for the first time, use the 'City Water' connections. Fresh water tank as well pump can be used as well. When filling, in order to let the air escape, turn on both the hot and cold water faucets until the water starts to flow steadily. Ensure all the pipes and faucets aren't leaking.

Inspect water heater drain plug, which is normally outside the RV, as well as the water heater over pressure safety valve to ensure they, too, aren't leaking. After the water starts to run steady, turn off the faucets and disconnect from the 'City Water' connections. Fill all the onboard tanks with fresh water. Again, open the hot and the cold faucets, and then close after the water flow has stopped. Turn on the fresh water pump. Immediately after it starts running, wait for some few minutes to hear if it cycles on again. If the pump doesn't cycle, then it is clear that the system is up and ready to be used. Although, if it cycles on, the indication is that there's either a leak or simply a pressure drop. Run sufficient water through each faucet to be sure that all RV antifreeze is cleared. This however, may not be an easy task. It is why you always need to consult a professional in case you aren't sure of what to do.

5) Liquid Propane (L.P)

Before you check your Liquid Propane, make sure that all its appliances as well as other items are turned off. Secondly, ensure that no open flames, smoking or sparks close to the area. Also, inside the RV, turn on the leak detector. Open the valve on your propane tanks to find out whether there's any leak. Soapy water helps much to detect leaks. You can use it to check for leaks around the valve and regulator. If by chance you detect any leak, quickly turn off the L.P valve and get a professional to handle it. Once again, do not try to do anything if you aren't sure.

6) Test fire appliances

After testing and ensuring that both the water and the L.P systems are ready for use, test the fire appliances. Light first the stove top burner if it's the first use ever. Turn the L.P gas leak detector, and then fill the lines. Light up another L.P fired item, e.g. the refrigerator. Fill the water heater with water before testing, and then ignite it.

7) Generator

In order to know and be sure that your generator is ready to be used, start it and check well if it functions. The problem however comes in when you want to start your generator after it has sat for a long time. When there's no fuel in the lines, it becomes very hard to start the generator. The prime feature in your generator will be very helpful in this stage. With the prime feature, you can prime the generator till the indicator light turns on for the fuel pump. Run the pump for a few seconds, to release the fuel to the carburetor. The generator at this stage will be able to start. If your generator does not have the prime feature, you'll have to crank it till it starts. After cranking for some few seconds, let the starter rest, then cycle it until it runs. Once you start it, let the generator run for a few minutes, then check its oil level. Also check the air filter to ensure that there aren't any nests from the storage.

8) Dump Hoses

Dump hoses' lifespan is always very short. Therefore, check your sewage dump hose to be certain that the hose is in a good state. Make sure also, before putting it to use, that it has no tears or holes.

9) Waste Tank Valve

Inspect the valve seal on the waste tank. Work out the handle in and out in short increments, to make sure that it opens and closes properly. Make sure the tank is empty before the inspection. Valve seals can at times dry out and become harder to operate. If it becomes hard, worry not. You can also purchase a valve lube in the parts department.

10) Awnings

Operate your awnings. To make sure that everything is intact, check for the holes, runs and tears. You can get a professional to help you work out your awnings, if it becomes difficult to operate.

Well, there you are! Planning an RV trip should now not be stressful, whether as a beginner or not. Simply set the trip, prepare your RV and enjoy the experience out there. You'll surely love it!

Conclusions

Being the first RV trip ever that I was going to have with my whole family, I always wished that it turns out well. And true to my wish, it turned out a beautiful and an amazing experience. We took some of the pictures, that have always reminded us of the awesome time we had then! To this day, my kids tell stories of their encounter in the first trip.

Well, RVing is all you need to do during the holidays. Just as I mentioned earlier, it lets you leave behind all your worries, leaving you refreshed and re-energized, ready to go through any season. It isn't any difficult to plan. A stitch in time, as they say, saves nine. Simply roll out your plans as early as possible, putting in place all the necessary basics. Also bear in mind some of the important factors such as weather conditions, which, if not well checked, can greatly affect your trip.

If you are looking forward to go for an RV trip and cannot afford an RV, simply rent one. Today, they are readily available everywhere and at very affordable prices. Depending on your needs, you can get an RV of any size that will accommodate all you have. Have also a professional with you to check all the parts necessary, so as not to give you a hard time when on the trip.

With all these, you can go ahead and give it a try.

Wish you well!

CPSIA information can be obtained
at www.ICGtesting.com
Printed in the USA
LVHW081323101120
671289LV00015B/558